What on Earth? Life in the Rainforest

What on Earth?

Dead

leaves?

D1344782

7000000298697

First published in 2005 by
Book House an imprint of
The Salariya Book Company
25 Marlborough Place
Brighton
BN1 1UB

© **The Salariya Book Company Ltd MMV**
All rights reserved. No part of this book may be reproduced, stored in a
retrieval system or transmitted in any form or by any means, electronic,
mechanical, photocopying, recording or otherwise, without the
written permission of the copyright owner.

HB ISBN 1-905087-39-X
PB ISBN 1-905087-40-3

Visit our website at **www.book-house.co.uk**
for free electronic versions of:
You Wouldn't Want to be an Egyptian Mummy!
You Wouldn't Want to be a Roman Gladiator!
Avoid joining Shackleton's Polar Expedition!
Avoid Sailing on a 19th-Century Whaling Ship!

Due to the changing nature of internet links, The Salariya Book Company
has developed an online list of websites related to the subject of this book.
This site is updated regularly. Please use this link to access the list:
http://www.book-house.co.uk/WOE/rainforest

A catalogue record for this book is available from the British Library.

Printed and bound in China.

Editor: Ronald Coleman
Senior Art Editor: Carolyn Franklin
DTP Designer: Mark Williams

Picture Credits Julian Baker: 8, 9, Carolyn Scrace: 1, 2, 3,
4, 6, 7, 8, 9, 13, 14, 16, 18, 19, 20, 21, 22, 23, Jordi Bas
Casas, NHPA: 10, 11, Jany Sauvanet, NHPA: 12, Kevin
Schafer, NHPA: 15, John Foxx: 13, 29, Digital Vision: 17,
28, DesignEXchange: 20, 24, PhotoDisc: 26, Corbis: 30, 31

What on Earth? **playing dead!**

Mantis

Dead leaf

This **mantis** hopes to fool its
predators by pretending it's
a dead leaf. If you don't look
good to eat - you
probably won't be eaten!

What on Earth?
Life in the
Rainforest

WRITTEN BY
KATHRYN SENIOR

ILLUSTRATED BY
CAROLYN SCRACE

Guess what this is?

Turn the page and find out!

BOOK HOUSE

Contents

What on Earth?

It's a pangolin!

A pangolin is easy prey but when in danger it rolls itself into a ball. Once rolled up, not even a leopard's strong claws can unroll it.

Introduction

Rainforests are wet most of the time. They are packed with many different kinds of life. Hundreds of **thousands** of insects, plant species, mammals, birds and amphibians jostle with each other for space. Rainforests are home to more than half the living species on Earth.

Why do plants grow so well there?

All of the world's rainforests are within a narrow band that stretches around the middle of the Earth. This area is warm and wet most of the time, which is why plants grow there so well. Rainforests used to cover about a **fifth** of the Earth's surface.

Why are rainforests so important?

Rainforests affect the world's weather. All trees release moisture into the air. If there are no trees to do this, rainfall levels drop and the world's **climate** changes. Yet as each year passes, more of the rainforests vanish as humans cut them down.

Rainforests

Rainforests are areas of dense tropical forest. Without trees there would be no rainforests, and without high rainfall and a hot steady temperature, there would be no trees to form a rainforest. Everything in the rainforest needs the trees. And trees need birds, animals and insects for pollination.

Red-eyed tree frog

Golden eyelash viper

Heliconid butterfly

Passion flower

Leaf-cutter ant

Poison-arrow frog

Oasis
hummingbird

Glass-wing
butterfly

Postman
butterfly

Tamandua and
its young

Tree porcupine

Squirrel monkey

Where in the world are rainforests?

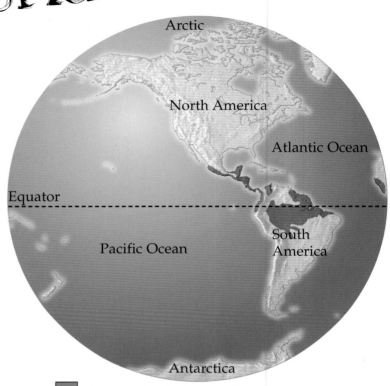

Rainforests occur in South America, Africa and Asia. Most of them lie between the tropics at the Equator, in the hottest part of the world. Rainforests need at least 200 cm (79 inches) of rainfall spread evenly throughout the year, and a temperature of 26°C (79°F). It is warmth and **dampness** that make the trees flourish.

Arctic

North America

Atlantic Ocean

Equator

Pacific Ocean

South America

Antarctica

☐ **Areas of rainforest shown on maps.**

How big are the rainforests in Africa?

The rainforest in West Africa and Madagascar covers 950,000 square kilometres (380,000 sq miles). These tropical forests are mainly in Zaire, Gabon, the Republic of the Congo, and the Central African Republic.

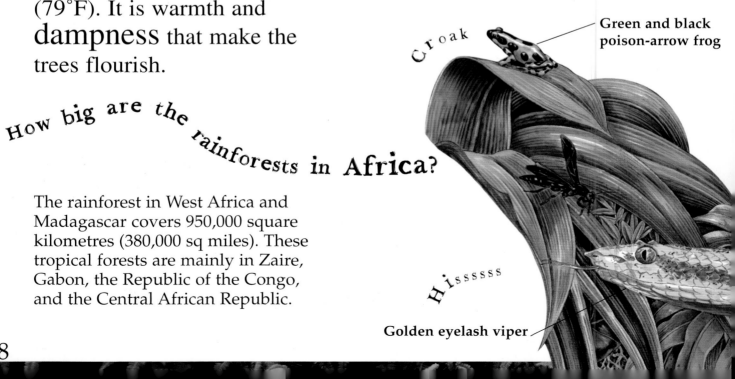

Croak

Green and black poison-arrow frog

Hisssssss

Golden eyelash viper

Where is the biggest rainforest?

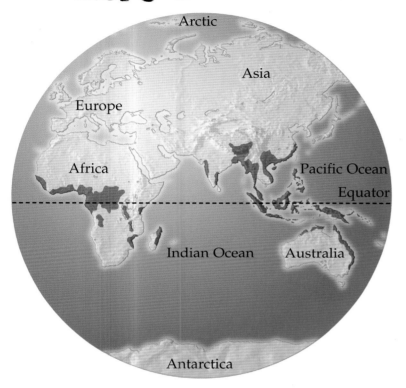

Arctic

Asia

Europe

Africa

Pacific Ocean

Equator

Indian Ocean

Australia

Antarctica

The largest lowland tropical rainforests are in northern and central South America which is home to over **half** the world's rainforests. Most of these forests are in Brazil, but Bolivia, Colombia, Ecuador, French Guiana, Guyana, Peru, Surinam, Venezuela and the republics of Central America all have some rainforest too.

Are all rainforests in the tropics?

Some rainforests lie outside of the tropics. These are called temperate rainforests. They are found on the north-west coast of North America, southern Chile, parts of south-eastern Australia and New Zealand. Where different types of rainforest meet, there is no clear boundary to mark the end of one and the beginning of another. They merge and change gradually over a large area.

What is the canopy?

A rainforest canopy, the area at the top of the trees, gets all the sun and rain. From above, the canopy looks like a solid green mass, stretching as far as the eye can see. Some rainforest trees are bigger and taller than trees found anywhere else in the world.

What is underneath the canopy?

The area under the canopy is called the understorey. Many trees in a rainforest have huge buttress roots that help support them as they grow. Below the understorey is the forest floor where dead leaves decay along with the remains of any animals. The soil is poor in the rainforest so it is important that everything rots down quickly to add nutrients to the soil.

Why are the leaves so big?

Tropical rainforest trees have really large leaves. They are usually about 20 cm (8 inches) long with very smooth edges which end in a sharp extended tip. This shape helps water run off the leaf easily.

What on Earth?

Jumping kangaroos!

The Goodfellows tree kangaroo travels through New Guinea's rainforests leaping up to 7 metres (22 feet) from one tree to another.

Harpy eagle

Rainforests are full of birds. Parrots are easy to spot because of their bright colours and loud calls. There are over 300 different types of parrot in the rainforests. They feed on seeds, grass, fruit, leaves and plant shoots. They use their strong beaks to **crack** hard shells, grind their food and to help them climb.

Sloth-eating eagle?

The harpy eagle is a large bird of prey, almost one metre (39 inches) long. It can pull some of the smaller apes and sloths out of trees with its huge claws.

Killer talons?

A harpy eagle has talons that are 12.5 cm (5 inches) long. They are as big as a grizzly bear's claws!

Cr0akkkkk! cr0akkkkk!

Sounds like a frog?

The keel-billed toucan's most obvious feature is its huge bill which is yellow, orange, red, green and black. It has a call which sounds like a frog croaking.

One of the largest parrots?

Macaws are one of the largest parrots in the rainforest. They live in Central and South America. They like to nest in holes in trees. Macaws are on the endangered species list because people catch them to sell as pets.

What on Earth?

Flying flat snakes!

Flying snakes live in South and South-East Asia. They jump from trees, flattening their entire body, and glide or parachute to the ground or another tree.

Don't look up!

13

What mammals live in trees?

Mammals are animals who are fed on their mother's milk when they are young. Mammals form a large part of the wildlife of the rainforest. Most of them live in the canopy and have special features to help them move easily from tree to tree. Many of the monkeys have **prehensile** tails. This means that their tails are very flexible and sensitive and can curl around and hang onto branches. It is a bit like having an extra arm.

Cotton-topped tamarin

A tiny monkey?

Tamarins are small monkeys weighing only about 500 g (one pound). Their main diet consists of insects, ripe fruit, seeds, nectar and gum that oozes from trees.

A squirrel monkey?

Squirrel monkeys are quite social animals and live in groups of about thirty. Several females in the group produce a single baby each year, all born around the same time.

slothing about?

Sloths (below) are so slow moving that they can be in the same tree for years! They live for about 30 years and may never see or walk on the forest floor at all.

Green sloth?

Algae grows on trees and even on some animals. Sloths can eventually turn a dull green colour because of the green algae growing on their fur!

15

Is there poison in the rainforest?

The rainforest of South America is home to many different types of poisonous frog. The frogs are quite small, the largest is no longer than 7 cm (3 inches). Males and females look much the same but the males have bigger **toe pads**. Toe pads have great suction power and the frogs use them to cling onto trees and branches.

Killer licks?

The frog's poison comes out of the pores of its skin. Even a lick can prove deadly to an unsuspecting animal that tries to eat it. This makes the frogs fearless. Amazingly one snake, named *leimadophis epinephelus*, seems to be unaffected by most poisonous frogs.

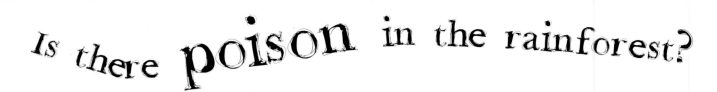

Dragonfly

Skeleton butterfly

Strawberry poison-arrow frog

Poison-arrow frog tadpoles

Day-flying clearwing moth

Why are frogs poisonous?

To stop other animals eating them! Poison frogs are always brightly coloured and can be easily seen by predators. They can be bright green, blue or red with lots of spots or markings. Animals learn to recognise these warning signs and stay well away.

What on Earth?

The deadliest poison?

One small frog can produce enough deadly venom (poisonous fluid) to load 50 poison-tipped arrows for hunting.

17

Are rainforests full of creepy-crawlies?

Rainforests are crawling with bugs. It is almost impossible to count every type of insect but experts guess that there are more than a million different kinds. Scientists believe that one hectare of the South American rainforest will contain 42,000 species of insect (including 50 different species of ant).

What is a hectare?

One hectare is 2.47 acres. It is about half the size of a football pitch.

Scissor mouths?

Ants are one of the most hard working insects in the rainforest. The leaf-cutter ant cuts up pieces of leaves with its scissor-like mouthparts.

Leaf or insect?

Many insects are well camouflaged. The katydid looks just like a leaf.

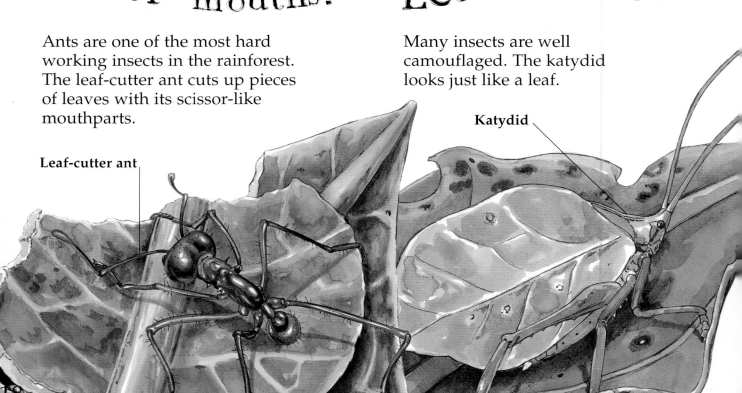

Katydid

Leaf-cutter ant

Too small to see?

Many insect species are too small to see. The hummingbird flower mite, for example is barely half a millimetre (0.01 inches) long. It is so small it can hitch a ride from flower to flower inside the nostril of a hummingbird.

Tadpoles in plants?

Water collects in the leaves of plants such as bromeliads where tree frogs lay their eggs.

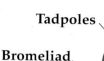

Tadpoles

Bromeliad

Green and black poison-arrow frog

Strawberry poison-arrow frog

What is the understorey?

The understorey is where tall shrubs and small trees grow. The growth of these young trees has been stunted by lack of sunlight. In the damp, dimly lit world of the understorey, mosses and algae flourish. They grow on trees, creepers and even on some animals. Fallen leaves that rot in the cracks in trees provide homes for worms and fungi.

What is an epiphyte?

An epiphyte (left) is a plant that grows on another plant. Epiphytes get water from raindrops trapped in their leaves, not through their roots as other plants do. It's also known as an 'airplant'.

Butterflies

Rainforests are home to many different species of butterfly. The rainforest in Costa Rica has over 1,000 separate species.

Ithomid butterfly

Spider monkey
with its young

Woolly monkey

Two-toed sloth
with its young

Marpesia
marcella
butterfly

Green-winged
macaw

What on Earth?

Howlerrrrr

The howler monkey has the **loudest** voice in the rainforest. They can be heard five kilometres (three miles) away!

Keep that noise down!

What lives on the forest floor?

Rainforest soil is very poor. The soil on the forest floor gets all its nutrients from 'forest litter'. This 'litter' of fallen trees and leaves and the remains of any dead creatures **decays** rapidly in the damp warm conditions. It turns into loose soft soil.

The forest floor is an ideal place for many creatures. Ants and termites make nests called 'castles' in the crumbly soil.

Deer and other mammals that cannot climb, feed on the shrubs. Can you spot the ocelot hidden on these pages?

Fallen tree trunk

Pit viper

Strawberry poison-arrow frog sitting on fungus

Litter frog

White-tailed deer

Cock-of-the-rock

Ocelot
Slender lizard

Coatimundi with its young

What on Earth?

Does your food come from the rainforest?

Do you eat tomatoes, corn, rice, coconuts, oranges, figs avocados, grapefruits, bananas, mangoes, guavas, chocolate, coffee, vanilla, black pepper, potatoes, cinnamon, ginger, cloves, cashews, brazil nuts, lemons, yams or sugar?

At least 3,000 fruits are found in the rainforest.

What is rainforest weather like?

A tropical rainforest is very hot and very wet. A typical day begins with a cloudless sky and a very light breeze. Even the temperature is pleasant. But during the morning, the temperature begins to rise and the rainforest gets hotter and hotter. It gets so hot, it starts to steam.

The steam turns into water vapour which becomes clouds. Around mid-afternoon, there is a stormy downpour that drenches the rainforest. Later in the afternoon, the temperature starts to go down again and the calm conditions of the morning return to the rainforest.

Walks on water?

The basilisk lizard of the South American rainforests is nicknamed the 'Jesus Christ lizard' because it can run on water.

Basilisks have large hind feet with flaps of skin between each toe. These web-like feet help them to run quickly across water.

Flying dragon?

The flying dragon doesn't really fly. It is a lizard found in the tropical forests of South East Asia. On either side of the lizard's body are thin, wing-like folds of skin. By extending its 'wings' it glides for distances of up to nine metres (30 feet) between trees.

Are rainforests under threat?

Yes, rainforests are under threat. Many countries with rainforests are poor. The governments see the forests as areas where nothing useful grows. They think the land should be used to rear cattle or grow crops. But the soil is shallow. If the trees are cut down, the soil will soon **wash** away. Where will the crops grow then? Even if crops are planted the soil is so poor that they do not grow well.

Once a forest?

Much of the African country of Ethiopia was originally tree-covered. Many areas were cleared of trees and suffered soil erosion. Drought and famine hit Ethiopia badly in the 1980s.

What on Earth?

HOW many trees can be cut down in a minute!

About 2,000 rainforest trees are cut down each minute. Mahogany and Rosewood are rainforest trees. They are cut down and made into furniture for **our** homes.

How would you survive in a rainforest?

People think of rainforests as dangerous places full of wild scary creatures. But really the most scary thing in the rainforest is probably you! You could get lost, fall down a ravine or drink bad water and become ill. If you want to stay fit and healthy – stick to paths, boil all drinking water and leave animals alone. Remember most animals are just like people – if you don't hurt them, they won't hurt you.

Rainforest Dangers

A king cobra has enough venom to kill up to 20 people in a single bite. But it only attacks in self defence or if its eggs are threatened, so if you see one leave it alone.

A tarantula is a spider which only attacks when upset. Its bite can be painful and cause swelling but no one has ever died of a tarantula bite.

A gorilla is a gentle and sociable herbivore who will only attack you if you threaten or confront it. Most gorillas get used to the presence of humans.

What to take Check-list

A **machete** so you can hack your way through the undergrowth. Wear sturdy **boots** and thick socks to avoid painful snakebites. Take some **salt** and if a leech tries to suck your blood, sprinkle some on it. Take some **tweezers** so you can remove ticks (small mites) and **antiseptic cream** to cover any wounds. Remember a **hammock** so you can sleep at night without fear of attack by bugs and other creatures.

Meat-eating plant?
Flies only, luckily for you... ARG!

The Venus flytrap lures its prey with its sweet smelling nectar. When an insect touches one of the hairs inside its jaws, they snap closed! Its victim is slowly dissolved!

Yum yummmmmm

Rainforest facts

The Amazon River basin in South America contains one fifth of all the fresh water on Earth.

Areas of rainforest the size of 2 American football fields disappear each second. Over one year the amount of rainforest being lost would cover about 26 million football fields.

Red-eyed tree frog

Approximately 50 million native people depend directly on tropical forests for shelter and food.

Over 90 different tribes from the Amazon rainforest are thought to have disappeared during the last 100 years.

On average rainforests have thunderstorms on about 200 days each year. The rest of the time it usually just rains, creating the very humid atmosphere of the tropical rainforest.

Deforestation accounts for the loss of nearly two-thirds of Central America's rainforests.

Tropical rainforests are so densely packed that rain falling on the canopy can take as long as ten minutes to reach the ground.

Glossary

Algae Simple water plants.

Buttress roots Roots growing from the sides of a tree down into the ground to give extra support.

Camouflage Markings or colouring on a creature that help it to blend with its surroundings.

Deforestation The cutting down, burning and removal of forests.

Endangered species A plant or animal in danger of disappearing forever.

Equator Imaginary line around the Earth's widest part.

Erosion Gradual wearing away of something.

Habitat The natural home of a plant or animal.

Herbivore An animal that only eats plants.

Paralyse To cause something to lose the power to move.

Pollination Exchange of pollen between flowering plants. Without pollination a flower cannot produce fruit and seeds.

Prey Creature that is hunted for food.

Species Group of plants or animals that look and behave alike.

Tropics Hot regions that lie north and south of the Equator.

Scarlet macaw

What do you know about rainforests?

1 Where are the tropics?

2 What is the area under the canopy called?

3 Which bird can sound like a croaking frog?

4 What has a prehensile tail?

5 Where might a sloth live for 30 years?

6 How many poison arrows can be made from from one frog's poison?

7 Does a tree frog lay its eggs in a plant?

8 Which monkey has the loudest call in the rainforest?

9 What is 'forest litter' in a rainforest?

10 How many trees are being cut down each minute in rainforests around the world?

Go to pages 32 for the answers!

Under threat?

Index

Pictures are shown in **bold** type.

Answers

1 Tropics are regions around the Equator. (See page 8)
2 The understorey. (See page 10)
3 The keel-billed toucan. (See page 13)
4 Many monkeys have prehensile tails. (See page 14)
5 In the same tree. (See page 15)
6 Fifty! (See page 17)
7 Yes. (See page 19)
8 The howler monkey. (See page 21)
9 Fallen trees, leaves, dead creatures. (See page 22)
10 About 2,000 trees a minute. (See page 26)

Yes

Orangutans live in the rainforests of Indonesia. They belong to the great ape family. These beautiful animals are under threat of extinction. Plantations to grow palm trees for extracting palm oil, illegal logging, tree clearance, mining and hunting are all responsible.